LONDON MIDLAND STEAM IN COLOUR

Hugh Ballantyne

Copyright © Jane's Publishing Company Limited 1984

First published in the United Kingdom in 1984 by
Jane's Publishing Company Limited
238 City Road, London EC1V 2PU

ISBN 0 7106 0309 6

Printed by Toppan Printing Co (S) Pte Ltd
38 Lui Fang Road, Jurong, Singapore 2262

JANE'S

Cover illustrations

Front: the first LMS Pacific, No 46200 *The Princess Royal*, built in
1933 and which gave its name to the class, makes a fine sight standing
in the sunshine at Crewe, preparing to leave for Euston with the
RCTS/SLS returning special 'Aberdeen Flyer' train. 3 June 1962.
(*Hugh Ballantyne*)
Voigtlander CLR   f2.8 Skopar   Agfa CT18   f8, 1/60

Back: Fowler-designed Class 4F 0–6–0 No 44123 coming up through
Berkeley Road station, junction for the Severn & Wye Joint line over
the Severn Bridge to Lydney, with a goods train heading towards
Gloucester. 4 June 1963. (*Hugh Ballantyne*)
Voigtlander CLR   f2.8 Skopar   Agfa CT18   f4, 1/250

Right: summer on Shap, and a welcome burst of sunlight breaks
between the rain clouds surging eastwards in the strong prevailing
south-westerly wind as 'Princess Coronation' class No 46238 *City of
Carlisle* passes the well-known but tiny signal box at Scout Green. The
maroon Pacific is working well up the 1 in 75 grade with the 'Lakes
Express', 11.35 am Euston to Workington. On the left is the
conspicuous up home signal with the repeater on the high post, which
was reputed to be the tallest in the Lancaster Division until its
replacement in 1963. 11 August 1962. (*Hugh Ballantyne*)
Voigtlander CLR   f2.8 Skopar   Agfa CT18   f4, 1/500

Introduction

This book sets out to portray some of the variety of locomotives which served the largest of the four British 'grouped' companies, the London Midland and Scottish Railway. Created by statute on 1 January 1923 and likewise destroyed by statute on 1 January 1948, the LMS thus enjoyed a mere 25 years of corporate existence. In 1923 the new company inherited a bewildering array of locomotives in all shapes and sizes, totalling 10 316 engines and comprising 393 different classes. Being the largest railway, it covered much of England, North Wales and Scotland, the latter from top to bottom, and by means of running powers and joint lines LMS engines penetrated right across East Anglia to Yarmouth, and to Bournemouth on the English Channel coast in the south.

With limitations of space in mind I have primarily concentrated on pictures of interesting engine classes rarely seen in colour, and then transparencies of the everyday working LMS engine on the system in England and Wales during BR operating days, when the major part of the LMS had become the London Midland Region. The constituent companies had produced Chief Mechanical Engineers of outstanding quality, or notoriety, and in the following pages you will find a representative selection of many of the locomotives designed by the LMS CMEs or some of their pre-grouping predecessors.

I would like to express my sincere gratitude to the photographers whose work appears in this book for their considerable generosity in allowing the Publishers and myself access to, and use of, their quite irreplaceable original and unpublished transparencies. To all of them I extend my thanks, and likewise to Andrew Biwandi and David Moore for providing certain detailed information for some of my picture captions.

Dedication

I dedicate this book to my wife, Toni, whose unfailing good humour and tolerance over the years has allowed me unlimited pleasure in my committed pursuit of photographing steam at work on BR and elsewhere around the world.

HUGH BALLANTYNE
Eccleshall, North Staffordshire
June 1984

An interesting study of two Stanier 'Princess Coronation' Pacifics facing each other at Kingmoor shed, Carlisle. On the left in BR lined green livery in No 46242 *City of Glasgow*, one of the engines involved in the terrible Harrow crash of October 1952, whilst on the right is No 46247 *City of Liverpool* in maroon. All the maroon-painted Pacifics were allocated to the London Midland Region. 6 April 1963. (*G W Morrison*)
Zeiss Contaflex   f2.8 Tessar   Agfa CT18

A most enterprising picture of Class 3P 2–6–2T No 40022 leaving Moorgate with the 5.11 pm suburban train for City workers via the Widened Lines to St Albans. This photograph was obtained by climbing onto scaffolding and taking the picture over a high wall during re-development of property in one of the world's most desirable real estate areas, and gives us an intriguing view of a Midland train at this Metropolitan station. Note the two distinctive 'Met' emu compartment stock trains in London Transport brown livery known as 'T Stock', all of which had disappeared by October 1962. Likewise No 40022, one of 70 engines designed by Fowler and built at Derby between 1930 and 1932, was the last of the class to be withdrawn in December 1962. 14 May 1959. (R C Riley)
Agfa Super Silette   f2 Solagon
Kodachrome 8 ASA   f2, 1/250

Left: The magnificent sight of a clean 'Princess Coronation' class Pacific, the pride of the line, sweeping down the West Coast Main Line near the site of Milford & Brocton station, four miles south-east of Stafford. Green–liveried No 46239 *City of Chester* has charge of the 12.55 (Sun) Euston to Blackpool and Barrow express. 14 September 1958. (*Michael Mensing*)
Solida III   f2.9 Radinar   Agfa CT18 f3.5, 1/500

Above: The last two 'Princess Coronation's' were built in 1947 and 1948 to the modified design of Mr H G Ivatt. New features included self-emptying ashpan, lighter cast steel pony truck, roller bearing on all axles and shortened cab side sheets which did not align with the bottom of the tender body. No 46256, built as No 6256 in December 1947, was the last constructed in LMS days and was very appropriately named *Sir William A Stanier FRS*. This fine engine was included with the last batch withdrawn, prematurely it seemed to many observers at the time, in October 1964, and to our everlasting regret was not saved for preservation. In this picture No 46256 is near the site of Milford & Brockton station, on the former LNWR main line, hauling an up fitted goods train towards the Trent valley area of Staffordshire. Circa 1960. (*J B Bucknall*)
Pentax S1   f2 Takumar   Agfa CT18

5

Rebuilt Patriot Class 5XP (later 6P) 4–6–0 No 45527 *Southport*, one of eighteen so treated by Mr H G Ivatt between 1946 and 1949 out of the Fowler class of 52 engines. Originally two had been built by Sir Henry Fowler in 1930, quickly followed by another 50 to supplement the 70 Royal Scots in the next power group and help relieve the desperate need of the LMS for a large fleet of competent modern express passenger engines. At the time the company found it was necessary to replace its hard-pressed life-expired four- and six-coupled 2-cylinder and 4-cylinder simples and compounds, due to their poor availability and expensive maintenance. No 45527, seen at Carlisle Upperby shed was named *Southport* in 1937, and was one of twelve engines in the class given names of resorts or holiday towns served by the LMS. It should have had an attractive civic coat arms above the nameplate in the blank space visible but it had been removed or stolen by the time this picture was taken. 30 August 1964. (*Hugh Ballantyne*)
Voigtlander CLR   f2.8 Skopar
Agfa CT18   f8, 1/60

Above: To provide a comparison with the rebuilt Patriot opposite you are invited to compare the very minor differences in this 'Converted Royal Scot' as in outline they look almost the same. Both the rebuilt 'Patriot' and the 'Converted Royal Scot' had the same taper 6A boiler and were power-rated by the LMS as Class 6P, becoming a post-war standard class. The differences visible are the cutaway cab with only one side window and the sandbox on the running plate above the rear driving wheel. No 46166 *London Rifle Brigade* was taken at Carlisle Kingmoor shed. 30 August 1964. (*Hugh Ballantyne*)
Voigtlander CLR   f2.8 Skopar
Agfa CT18   f8, 1/60

Right: The 'Royal Scots' were mainly named after regiments of the British army and carried elegant nameplates on the leading splasher. Some plates had double-line lettering and many had a fine regimental badge, beautifully detailed, as seen in this picture of the right side nameplate of No 46166 taken at Willesden shed. 18 August 1963. (*Rodney Lissenden*)
Rolliflex 4 × 4   f3.5 Xenar
Agfa CT18

Passengers Cross
The Line By The
Footbridge Only

Left: A rural scene at the single platform of Uppingham station, terminus of a short 3¾ miles-long branch of the former LNWR from Seaton, a delightful little market town in what was then England's smallest county, Rutland. On the railway map the LNWR pushed eastwards across the heart of the Midland Railway's territory from Rugby towards Peterborough and this was one of two branches off that line from Seaton. In later days LMS-built Tilbury type Class 3P 4–4–2Ts emigrated north to Spital Bridge shed at Peterborough to help work the service, as seen here with No 41975, until the

last year or so when Ivatt Class 2 2–6–2Ts took over completely. The branch was closed in June 1960. June 1959. (*D A Soggee*)
Agfa Silette   *f2.8 lens*   *Kodachrome 8 ASA*

Right: The other branch of the LNWR from Seaton went 3¾ miles eastwards to Luffenham Junction where it met the Midland to go six miles further on to Stamford, just over the border in Lincolnshire. In the 1960s the service was worked by push-pull-fitted Ivatt Class 2s or BR Standard light 2–6–2Ts based at Market Harborough. This continued until 4 October

1965 to become the last steam-operated push-pull service in the country. The replacement DMU-only lasted eight months and the Luffenham–Seaton section was closed to all traffic on 6 June 1966. This picture shows Ivatt 2–6–2T No 41212 propelling its train out of Stamford station, in an attractive setting of flower beds and a lovely Midland Railway home signal, with the 10.15 to Seaton, three weeks before replacement. 16 September 1965. (*Hugh Ballantyne*)
Voigtlander CLR   *f2.8 Skopar*
Agfa CT18   *f4, 1/60*   9

To many people No 6100 *Royal Scot* was the flag bearer of the former LMS fleet and here is a fine portrait of it taken at Aston shed, Birmingham, in its converted form with taper boiler as BR No 46100. This engine was in fact built as No 6152 *The King's Dragoon Guardsman* at Derby in 1930 and switched identities with the original No 6100, built in 1927 by North British Locomotive Co, in 1933. That year the LMS sent an engine No 6100 to the United States to be exhibited at the Chicago 'Century of Progress' exhibition, but it has not been substantiated which of the two engines was the one that actually made the journey. However, the identities never reverted back and the later No 6100 had a commemorative plate added below the nameplate which it carried for the rest of its working life. The engine was fitted with a 2A boiler in 1950 and was withdrawn in 1962. It is now preserved at Bressingham, near Diss, Norfolk. 1 October 1961. (*T B Owen*)

Leica M2   f2 Summicron   Kodachrome II f4.5, 1/125

The last 'Converted Royal Scot' in service was No 46115 *Scots Guardsman*, seen here coming off Crewe North shed as the sun rose on a cold February morning prior to proceeding to the station to work the 'Commemorative Scot' tour organised by the RCTS to Carlisle via the Settle & Carlisle route. Five of the class survived until 1965 and No 46115, the last, was officially withdrawn from Carlisle Kingmoor shed in December of that year. It is now preserved at Dinting, near Glossop. 13 February 1965. (*Hugh Ballantyne*)
Voigtlander CLR   f2.8 Skopar
Agfa CT18

Right: One of the former North Staffordshire Railway sheds, Stoke on Trent, 1935 LMS shed code 5D, which lasted as a steam depot until the penultimate year of steam on BR, 1967. By the time this picture was taken in August 1966 the rundown scene with dirt and general neglect, both with regard to the shed facilities and in the array of Class 8Fs, BR Standard Class 4 4–6–0s and Stanier Class 5s, is sadly very evident. August 1966. (*J B Bucknall*)
Pentax S1   f2 Takumar   Agfa CT18

Opposite: Scene at Carlisle Upperby shed, with three of the prolific Fowler-designed standard Class 3F shunting 0–6–0Ts prominent in the foreground. In all 422 engines of this type were built between 1924 and 1931 as a slightly modernised version of an already proven Midland Railway design. All except the last fifteen, which were constructed at Horwich, were built by five private contractors. In this picture are, left to right, No 47614 (Beardmore, 1928), No 47288 (North British, 1924) and No 47667, one of the last batch company-built at Horwich. Also clearly visible is a small design feature, the 'key hole' in the bottom of the side tanks on the left and right members of the trio. Contrary to driver's tales, this was not for winding up the clockwork mechanism, but the means of access to the sand box filler! The engine in the middle without the 'key hole' has its filler cap in the top of the side tank, necessitating the sand going down a pipe inside the tank to the sand container situated below the footplating. Behind the 0–6–0Ts can be seen No 46455 on the left, No 46200 *The Princess Royal* in faded maroon livery and No 45545 *Planet*, both the latter stored out of service. 12 September 1964. (*Hugh Ballantyne*)
Voigtlander CLR   f2.8 Skopar
Agfa CT18   f8, 1/60

Right: A view of Lostock Hall shed, a former Lancashire & Yorkshire Railway depot on the south side of Preston, taken from the south-west showing in front of the eight-road building (*l to r*) No 45149, No 43027, No 44878, No 48620, Class 08 diesel shunter and No 44713 (with Nos 48410 and 48715 behind). In LMS days under the 1935 shed code scheme this depot was designated 23E, later becoming 24C and finally in September 1963 recoded 10D. Lostock Hall survived until the very end of steam on BR and finally closed as a steam depot on 5 August 1968. 12 April 1968. (*Hugh Ballantyne*)
Voigtlander CLR   f2.8 Skopar
Agfa CT18   f8, 1/60

The final development of LMS express locomotive design was Mr W A Stanier's 'Princess Coronation' class Pacifics. A total of 38 were built, commencing in 1937, the year of the Coronation of His Majesty King George VI, hence the class name. Of these 24 were streamlined and 14 non-streamlined, although all the former were 'de-streamlined' after the war, the last so fitted being No 46243 *City of Lancaster* in 1949. This portrait shows No 46250 *City of Lichfield*, one of the wartime-built non-streamlined batch in 1944, at the north end of Shrewsbury station on a train to Crewe, probably a running in turn as the engine appears in ex-works condition. Circa 1960. (*Basil Roberts*) *Kodak Retinette 1B   Agfa CT18*

A fine portrait of the Carlisle Upperby main line stand-by locomotive showing the immaculate condition in which this shed kept its namesake 'Princess Coronation' No 46238. The engine is seen painted in the maroon livery applied by the London Midland Region to 20 Pacifics during 1957–58, a small gesture well received by public and enthusiasts alike. This picture should be compared with that opposite as two minor differences can be seen; the shape of the smoke deflectors and the LMS post-war practice of discarding the fall plate of the running plate in front of the cylinders on the de-streamlined locos (except No 46242) and all the post-war-built engines. This small point of design seemed at the time to the author to be a somewhat unsightly economy which should have only been permitted on overseas or austerity locomotives! Certainly the succeeding BR management thought so too, as all the later BR Standards were suitably covered in. 13 June 1964. (*Rodney Lissenden*)

Rolliflex 4 × 4   f3.5 Zenar   Agfa CT18

A sad sight appeared at Bath shed yard one fine summer evening in 1962, when the very last of a long line of Somerset & Dorset, Midland and LMS-built inside cylinder 4–4–0s ceased work in the area. This Class 2P, No 40537, one of a series originated by Mr S W Johnson in 1882 and subsequently rebuilt by Deeley and Fowler, was en route light engine from Templecombe to Derby for scrapping. It stayed overnight at Bath and continued on its melancholy journey north- wards early next morning. 22 August 1962. (*Hugh Ballantyne*)
Voigtlander CLR   f2.8 Skopar
Agfa CT18   f4, 1/60

An action picture of one of the most famous pre-Second World War LMS engines, a Class 4P Compound 4–4–0. During 1923, the first year of the newly created LMS, the only new passenger tender engines put into service were Hughes 4-cylinder 4–6–0s, and towards the end of the year dynamometer car trials took place over the Settle & Carlisle line using a superheated Compound, a Class 999 4–4–0 and 'Prince of Wales' 4–6–0. No 1008, the selected Compound, ably demonstrated its ability to handle economically really heavy trains over this formidable route and consequently the company decided to build 195 more Compounds to supplement the original 45 Midland Railway Johnson/Deeley engines. For their size, they performed yeoman service until after nationalisation, when they were displaced by BR Standard types particularly in power Class 4. No 41157 was built by North British in 1925 and by the time this picture was taken of her leaving Derby in 1959 with the 5.30 pm (Sun) train to Nottingham, only eleven remained. Exactly one year later this engine was withdrawn, and the final two were scrapped in 1961. 25 May 1959. (R C Riley)
Agfa Super Silette   f2 Solagon
Kodachrome 8 ASA   f2, 1/250

Left: Activity in Bristol LMS shed yard as Fowler Class 4F No 44092 draws out the little 'Pug' 0–4–0ST Class 0F No 51218 towards Barrow Road Bridge, which bisected the shed yard. This depot had amongst its allocation two ex-L & Y 'Pugs' which were used for shunting the restricted Avonside Wharf branch. In LMS days the shed was coded 22A but in BR times it became known, appropriately, as Barrow Road and when placed under Western Region jurisdiction, coded 82E. The shed finally closed in October 1965 and was the last of the three sheds in the city of Bristol. 5 October 1962. (*R C Riley*)
Agfa Super Silette   f2 Solagon
Kodachrome II   f4, 1/250

Above: Dawn is breaking at Bristol Temple Meads station, where Stanier-designed Class 5 No 44941 stands at platform 6, having just taken over a northbound West of England to Derby train from a Western Region 'Castle'. This Stanier class was numerically the second largest constructed since the grouping on the former LMS system, 842 having been built, a figure only exceeded by the same designer's Class 8F 2–8–0 goods, engine which totalled ten more, although not all of those worked in this country. This particular locomotive was one of a group built at Horwich in 1945 and was withdrawn in 1966. 28 July 1962. (*Peter W Gray*)
Agfa Super Silette   Kodachrome II
f2, 20 secs

Above: A portrait of Class 2F 0–6–0T No 51537, one of a small and camera-shy class of Lancashire & Yorkshire locomotives latterly used in Liverpool docks; this photograph was taken at Bankfield Goods, near the Alexandra and Canada Dock. This engine was the last survivor of 20 Aspinall engines of LYR Class 24 built at Horwich in 1897. These outside-cylinder engines had a modified form of Allan link motion with curved links and this particular locomotive had flangeless centre coupled wheels for working on the sharply curved dockside lines. Scrapping of the class commenced as long ago as 1917 and only five passed into BR ownership on 1 January 1948. This engine was withdrawn in October 1961 from Aintree shed. 11 April 1959. (*R C Riley*)
Agfa Super Silette   f2 Solagon

Kodachrome 8 ASA   f8, 1/60

Right: Scene at Liverpool Exchange station showing an unkempt Class 5 No 44950 about to draw out the stock of the 16.53 from Preston to Liverpool train to Kirkdale carriage sidings. 19 May 1968. (*J E Berry*)

Above: An LMS train heading for Paddington! On the former GWR/LNWR Birkenhead joint line to Chester, Stanier Class 4 2-cylinder 2–6–4T No 42613 slows for the stop at Hooton with the 2.35 pm Birkenhead–Paddington train. This was the only intermediate stop on the Wirral, but the train had many more stops to make before reaching the capital, plus engine changes at Chester and Shrewsbury, which meant the big 2–6–4T would only run the first 15 miles of the journey to Chester. 20 August 1966. (*Hugh Ballantyne*)
Voigtlander CLR   f2.8 Skopar
Agfa CT18   f4, 1/500

Right: A dirty Stanier Class 5 No 45298 approaching the western end of the LNWR/GWR joint station at Chester with a Llandudno to Liverpool train, snaking over the points and under two of the magnificent LNWR signal gantries controlled by the big LNWR style signal boxes strategically placed in the area. Behind the first coach part of Chester No 4 box can be seen whilst to the right, partly visible, is the former GWR loco shed, which by the time the picture was taken had become a DMU depot. 20 August 1966. (*Hugh Ballantyne*)
Voigtlander CLR   f2.8 Skopar
Agfa CT18   f5.6 1/250

22

Left: BR Standard Class 7 Pacific No 70001 *Lord Hurcomb* lays a trail of black smoke over the Warwickshire countryside as it pounds down the West Coast Main Line through Polesworth with a parcels train. Today the station is still open and the LNWR-style signal box seen between the up and down lines remains in use. 4 June 1963. (*Hugh Ballantyne*)
Voigtlander CLR
f2.8 Skopar
Agfa CT18
f2.8–4, 1/500

Opposite: 'Jubilee' Class 4–6–0 No 45595 *Southern Rhodesia* going well on an up parcels train from Crewe to Euston, east of Shrugborough tunnel, where the West Coast Main Line comes into the Trent valley and meets the Stoke line at Colwich. The engine was distinctive in that it was one of only three 'Jubilees' to have a badge over the nameplate, clearly seen here, a pleasant addendum complementing the name, and frequently used by the LMS on engines in the 'Patriot' and 'Royal Scot' classes. Circa 1960.
(*J B Bucknall*)
Pentax S1
f2 Takumar
Agfa CT18

25

Left: Maximum effort climbing 'The Long Drag' as two Stanier Class 8F 2–8–0s battle up the 1 in 100 gradient towards Ribblehead station with 1000 tons of rails, northbound for track renewals circa 1966. *(F G Cronin)*
Zeiss Werra 1
f2.8 Tessar
Agfa CT18

Opposite: Super-power coming along the up slow at Madeley on the West Coast Main Line as Class 8Fs Nos 48074 and 48398 in tandem, get into their stride with a heavy goods train south of Crewe. At the time both locomotives were allocated to Nuneaton shed and No 48074 was one of the 8Fs which was fitted with dual brake valves, giving the driver the benefit of an independent brake control for use when running light engine. 20 May 1961. *(Hugh Ballantyne)*
Voigtlander CLR
f2.8 Skopar
Agfa CT18
f2.8–4, 1/1500

Left: The author recalls that when making visits to Crewe Works in steam days photography was strictly prohibited inside buildings and workshops, much to his dismay. However, on this occasion the photographer appears to have the blessing of the party guide, who can be seen sitting smiling at the camera in the impressive main erecting shop where, amongst others, Ivatt

Class 2 2–6–0 No 46416, a BR Standard Class 9F and an LMS Class 5 are receiving attention. Circa 1960. (*J B Bucknall*)
Pentax S1   f2 Takumar   Agfa CT18

Above: The finished product after repair from the workshops opposite. One of Sir Henry

Fowler's Class 5XP 'Patriots', No 45506 *The Royal Pioneer Corps*, built here in 1932, stands outside the works. This engine was in service for 30 years, but did not receive its name until 1948. 27 May 1956. (*T B Owen*)
Leica 3c   f2 Summitar
Kodachrome 8 ASA   f3.5, 1/60

29

On the former LNWR it would seem that for a while when Mr F W Webb was its CME, he may have seen merit in the GWR's idea of providing tank locomotives with pannier tanks rather than the more conventional side or saddle tanks, as several tank classes were built or rebuilt at Crewe with pannier tanks. This is a very rare colour photograph of No 47862, an attractive little 0-4-2PT, which was one of a class of 20 which first appeared in 1896 for shunting duties. Another unusual feature was that they had Bissel pony trucks with very small disc wheels, clearly visible in this picture. Only two survived long enough to be nationalised in 1948 and this one, seen as a works shunter at Crewe was not only the last of the class, withdrawn in November 1956, but also the last LNWR shunter at the works. 27 May 1956. (*T B Owen*)

Leica 3c   f2 Summitar
Kodachrome 8 ASA   f3.5, 1/60

One of the 230 Lancashire & Yorkshire Railway 0–6–0STs which saw service all over that compact system, seen very much on its home territory at Sowerby Bridge shed. No 51381 had been built as an 0–6–0 to the 1877 Class F16 design of W Barton Wright and was later rebuilt by Aspinall as an 0–6–0ST, as seen here. During LMS/BR days it was Class 2F and the last of the type was withdrawn in 1964, some examples having worked out their careers pottering about at Crewe as works shunters. One, LYR No 752, is preserved on the Keighley & Worth Valley Railway. 3 April 1955. (*T B Owen*)

Leica 3c   f2 Summitar
Kodachrome 8 ASA   f3.5, 1/60

31

Above: An extremely dirty large Fowler Class 4 2–6–4T No 42301, the second of the class, leaving Carnforth with the 7.00 pm to Leeds. The coaches of this train were added to the rear of the 5.35 pm from Heysham at Wennington, which then continued as one train through to Leeds City station, arriving at 9.23 pm. This locomotive was one of 125 very successful passenger tank engines to the design of Sir Henry Fowler and all built at Derby between 1927 and 1934.

They had all been withdrawn by 1966 and unfortunately none have been preserved. 3 July 1964. *(N A Machell)*
Zeiss Werra   f2.8 Tessar   Agfa CT18
f4, 1/250

Right: The BR lined black livery suits the big Fowler 2–6–4T No 42417 as she is caught in the afternoon sunlight leaving Birmingham New Street station with the 12.15 pm local train to

Worcester Shrub Hill. If you compare this engine with that opposite you will notice the cab shape is quite different and this is explained by the fact that the final batch were built after Stanier had become CME and he fitted them with side-window cabs of a type which appeared on subsequent Stanier 2–6–4Ts. 4 March 1961. *(R C Riley)*
Agfa Super Silette   f2 Solagon
Kodachrome 8 ASA   f2, 1/250

Above: At a distant outpost of its parent Midland Railway this little 0–4–0T designed by R M Deeley, No 41535, is being coaled from an open 16-ton wagon in the shed yard of Swansea East Dock, a former Great Western shed, in May 1964. This engine was used both as a shed pilot and for shunting in Swansea South Docks, hence the warning bell for dock work, clearly visible in front of the cab. Within a month of this photograph the shed closed and No 41535 made a short move to Llandore shed. This proved of brief duration as the little engine was withdrawn in September 1964. 19 May 1964. (*Hugh Ballantyne*)
Voigtlander CLR   *f2.8 Skopar*
Agfa CT18   *f11, 1/30*

Right: One of ten small Class 0F 0–4–0STs, No 47005, seen in clean condition shunting at Staveley Works, a few miles north-east of Chesterfield. Five locomotives were built by Kitson's for the LMS in 1932, while a further five were included in the 1953–54 BR construction programme and it fell to Horwich works to build them. This one was the first of the London Midland Region quintet outshopped in October 1953 and put to work from Birkenhead shed. It was withdrawn in 1966, the same year as the remaining class survivors. 9 May 1964. (*G W Morrison*)
Zeiss Contaflex   *f2.8 Tessar*   *Agfa CT18*

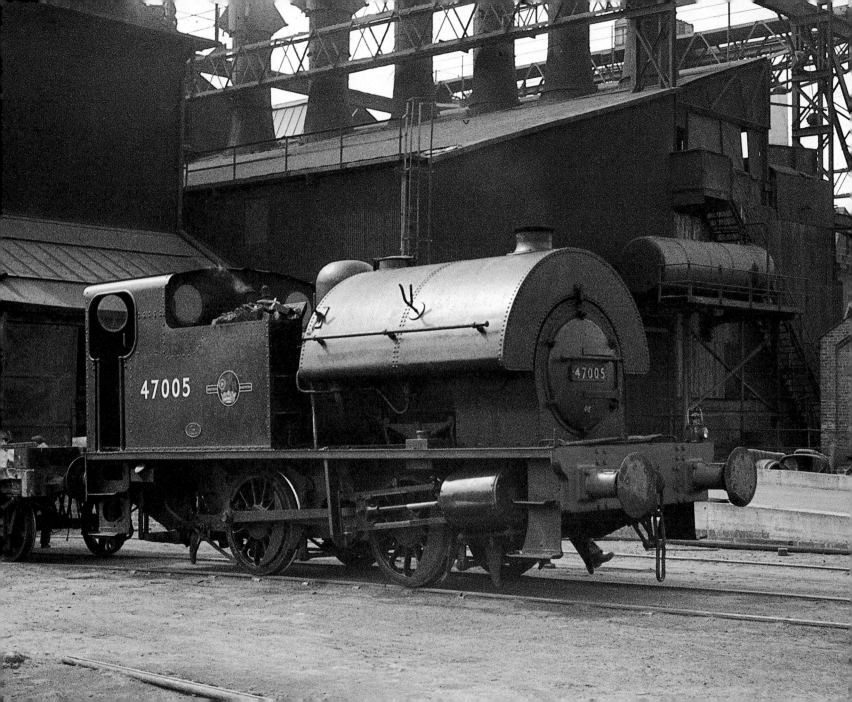

Left: At the summit of the LNWR main line linking Lancashire and Yorkshire and having topped the 1 in 105 gradient above Marsden on the climb from Huddersfield, Stanier Class 8F No 48765 is just about to enter Standedge tunnel, at 3 miles 60 yards the second longest of the four trans-Pennine tunnels, with a coal train from Healey Mills yard to the Manchester area. In the foreground can be seen the disused tracks leading to the two single line tunnels, which were opened respectively in 1849 and 1871 and closed on 30 October 1966. September 1967. *(F G Cronin)*
Zeiss Werra I   *f2.8 Tessar*   *Agfa CT18*

Above: A fine view in the heart of the Derbyshire Peak District at Millers Dale, showing Class 5 No 45057 coming south with an up cement train. This beautiful line, now closed, formed part of the Midland Railway main line to Manchester from Derby and London. 18 September 1965. *(John H Dagley-Morris)*
Kodak Retinette   *Agfa CT18*   *f6.5, 1/250*

37

Left: This attractive little Class 2F 2–6–0 designed by the last CME of the LMS, H G Ivatt, was another of the eleven LMS standard classes and 128 of this type were built between 1946 and 1953. Here No 46440, built at Crewe in 1950, heads into the evening sunshine past Pinfold crossing box at Uttoxeter, on the North Staffordshire Railway's line towards Stoke-on-Trent, with a short parcels train. 19 August 1961. (*Michael Mensing*)
Hasselblad 1000F   f2.8 Tessar
Agfa CT18   f4, 1/250

Opposite: The Midland Railway made territorial intrusions into Wales, albeit for only a short distance on its own metals. Its branch from Hereford along the upper reaches of the River Wye to Three Cocks Junction, a distance of 26¾ miles, enabled contact to be made with the Cambrian. By means of running powers the Midland then reached Brecon and eventually Ynis-y-Geinon near Bryn Amman where it owned more trackage in its own right on to Swansea. In later days of operation in this area the light Class 2 2–6–0s designed by H G Ivatt worked many of the services, as seen here with No 46511 (built at Crewe in 1947) entering Three Cocks with the 4.07 pm train from Hereford to Brecon. This line and many others serving Brecon and Central Wales suffered the ultimate fate at the hands of the infamous British Railways Board Chairman, Beeching, and was closed with effect from 29 December 1962, just at the start of a long and cold winter freeze. 31 August 1962. (*Alan Wild*)
Kodak Retinette 1A   Perutz C18

Above: One of the distinctive large Class 5F Moguls No 42769, allocated to Northwich but basking in the evening sunlight outside Warrington Dallam shed. This locomotive was one of 245 2–6–0s designed by the first CME of the LMS, George Hughes, although the first were not completed until after his retirement in 1926 by which time Sir Henry Fowler had taken charge. They were the first pure LMS design and as can be seen here were of notable appearance with conspicuously inclined cylinders, high running plate and spacious cab. They proved satisfactory engines in service and two survived until 1967, this particular machine having been built at Crewe in 1927 and withdrawn in 1964. 24 August 1963. (*Hugh Ballantyne*)
Voigtlander CLR   f2.8 Skopar
Agfa CT18   f5.6, 1/60

Right: On a sunny autumn day 'Converted Royal Scot' No 46122 *Royal Ulster Rifleman* is slowing for the Cheltenham Lansdown station stop with a Sheffield to Bristol train, while Hughes Mogul No 42790 stands in a loop at Alstone sidings at the head of a down goods train. 3 November 1961. (*John H Dagley-Morris*)
Agfa Silette   Agfa CT18   f9, 1/125

Above: On a sunny evening Stanier Class 8F No 48750 simmers gently on Willesden shed. This was a major LMS shed situated in north-west London, primarily for freight locomotives, and coded 1A from 1935. The 8F, which is being kept company by Class 5 No 44800 outside the 1929-built roundhouse, was from Westhouses shed and was photographed only a month after heavy overhaul at Crewe, hence its clean condition, albeit slightly marred by the rusty smoke box door handrail. Note the five-pointed white star below the number on the cabside which denotes that the engine is one of the class which has had its wheels balanced to enable it to work fitted freight trains. 10 June 1964. (*Hugh Ballantyne*)
Voigtlander CLR   f2.8 Skopar
Agfa CT18   f8, 1/60

Right: 'Jubilee' class 4–6–0 No 45633 *Aden* raises the echoes in the suburbs of north-west London at Kensal Green as the filthy engine gets an overnight fast fitted goods away from Camden and heads northwards into the late evening sunlight. This engine was one of five of the 191 Jubilees to be renamed, having originally been called *Trans-Jordan* until becoming *Aden* in September 1946. 14 May 1964. (*Hugh Ballantyne*)
Voigtlander CLR   f2.8 Skopar
Agfa CT18   f2.8, 1/500

42

Left: A good action picture of one of the 842 Stanier-designed Class 5 mixed traffic 4–6–0s, No 44679, which was built at Horwich in 1950, pounding up the West Coast Main Line near Cheddington with a train to Euston. This locomotive was one of eight built with Skefco roller bearings on all axles, but even so it had a life of only 17 years, as it was withdrawn in 1967. 8 September 1962. *(Rodney Lissenden)*
Rolleicord Vb   f3.5 Xenar Agfa CT18

Opposite: More Class 5 action, this time on the Midland Railway main line where No 44667, built at Crewe in 1949, is climbing the 1 in 119 rise near Sharnbrook summit, north of Bedford, with a down afternoon train from St Pancras. Note the non-corridor coaches, in particular the different livery of the second vehicle, which is still painted red as used in earlier BR days to distinguish suburban or local stock from main line coaches. Further back there are two coaches in the red and cream livery of main line stock which preceded the maroon colour scheme eventually used for all types of passenger stock except those on the Southern Region. 30 August 1958. *(T B Owen)*
Leica 3c   f2 85 mm Sonnar Kodachrome 8 ASA f2.8, 1/200

Aesthetically I consider that all the locomotives designed by Sir William Stanier, as be became in 1944, were well proportioned and generally very handsome. Unquestionably the LMS board did much for their company by obtaining Stanier in 1932 from the GWR, where at Swindon he had been Mr Collett's Principal Assistant and important member of the CME's staff. The 'Princess Coronation' Pacifics, introduced in streamlined form in 1937, were his masterpiece and eventually 38 were built over eleven years. By 1949 the last of the 24 streamliners had their casing removed and here one of the de-streamlined engines, No 46240 *City of Coventry*, makes a splendid sight in maroon livery harmonising with its stock, coming round the curves near Baswich on the approach to Stafford with a down express from Euston about 1960. (*J B Bucknall*)

Pentax S1   f2 Takumar   Agfa CT18

Again admire the pleasing lines of a BR green-liveried 'Princess Coronation' No 46241 *City of Edinburgh* as she gets into her stride up the 1 in 98 southbound climb out of Lancaster Castle station towards Lancaster No 1 Box with the Saturdays-only Dundee to Manchester and Crewe train. This engine was built in streamlined form in 1940, de-streamlined in 1947 and withdrawn in 1964. 20 July 1963. (*N A Machell*)
Zeiss Werra   f2.8 Tessar   Agfa CT18
f5.6, 1/250

The LNWR had a beautiful branch of 39¾ miles length from Penrith to Workington which traversed the heart of Cumberland, passing Keswick and skirting the west side of Bassenthwaite Lake, known as the Cockermouth, Keswick & Penrith line. Cockermouth is an old market town at the confluence of the Rivers Derwent and Cocker and birthplace of William Wordsworth in 1770. Once it had an attractive station, as evidenced here, where passengers are seen picking up their luggage to join the approaching up 'Lakes Express', on the first stages of its journey from Workington to Euston. The train engine, Ivatt Class 2F 2–6–0 No 46432 will only work the train as far as Penrith, where the train reverses before heading south. The branch west of Keswick was closed to all traffic on 16 April 1966, and subsequently the whole branch has vanished. 21 August 1964. (*D Cross*)
Canon VT6
f1.2 Canon lens

Further east along the same branch, with the mass of Saddleback rising to 2847 feet in the background, No 46432 again brings a Workington to Penrith train towards Troutbeck station. 1 July 1964. (*Rodney Lissenden*)
Rolleiflex 4 × 4
f3.5 Xenar   Agfa CT18

51

Ex-Midland Railway Class 1F 0–6–0T No 41734 blows off steam during a pause in shunting operations at Staveley Iron & Chemical Co's works in Derbyshire, while the shunter and locomotive crew await further instructions. This lovely old engine was one of the last five of the type and had been used under an Agreement of 1866 between the Iron company and the Midland for the railway to supply locomotives to shunt the works sidings for one hundred years. This engine was one of 137 locomotives built by Mr S W Johnson between 1878 and 1892 and known as the '1377' class. One of the Staveley survivors, No 41708, with original open back cab, is preserved on the Keighley & Worth Valley Railway. 5 March 1961. (*R C Riley*)

Agfa Super Silette   f2 Solagon
Kodachrome 8 ASA   f8, 1/60

A later Midland 0–6–0T Class 3F designed by Johnson appeared in 1899 and 60 were built. They were subsequently rebuilt by Mr Fowler with Belpaire boilers and improved cabs and formed the basis for the almost identical shunting Class 3F 0–6–0Ts constructed by the LMS from 1924. Here one of the Midland engines, No 47236, stands by the coaling stage at Horninglow shed in Burton-on-Trent. This town, just in Staffordshire, was deep in the heart of Midland territory, but this shed was owned by the LNWR, who successfully made a territorial invasion into the other LMS constituent company's area. The shed was closed in September 1960. Note the substantial malthouses, now demolished, but evidence of Burton's importance then, as now, as one of the major brewery towns in England. 28 September 1957. (R C Riley)

Agfa Super Silette   f2 Solagon
Kodachrome 8 ASA   f8, 1/60

Left: A busy scene at the most southerly point of the LMS system. This was Bath, an historic city situated in the north-east corner of Somerset and served by the Midland Railway on a branch from Mangotsfield off the Birmingham to Bristol line. The shed, LMS 1935 code 22C, was used by both the Midland and the Somerset & Dorset, the former having a small stone-built shed in the top yard and the latter the wooden four-road building just visible on the left of the picture. Except on summer Saturdays Bath LMS led a very quiet life so far as passenger traffic was concerned, but at holiday times it was busy and congested due to the limited facilities available at its terminus station. In this picture, taken on a peak summer Saturday every engine in view is of a different class. Left to right: a Class 4F 0–6–0; Class 7F No 53807 with No 46147 *The Northamptonshire Regiment* behind; Class 5 No 44853; Standard Class 4 No 75072 piloting the 9.08 am Birmingham–Bournemouth West out of the station; Ivatt Class 4 No 43012 and 'Jubilee' Class No 45682 *Trafalgar* waiting to leave with a train going northwards off the Somerset & Dorset line. 21 July 1962. (*Hugh Ballantyne*)

Voigtlander CLR   f2.8 Skopar
Agfa CT18   f8, 1/60

Above: Little was I to know when I took this photograph that ten years later, and following withdrawal by BR in March 1964, this loco-motive would be resurrected from the scrapyard at Barry, restored to working order, resplendent in pre-war LMS maroon livery, and passed for running on selected BR lines. Here No 45690 *Leander* in everyday BR working condition has made the short journey over from Bristol Temple Meads to Bath Green Park with the 8.50 am Whit Monday holiday excursion train to Bournemouth West, and is seen on the Cowans Sheldon-built turntable at Bath shed, being turned prior to running light engine back to its home depot at Bristol, thus to complete a very modest morning's work. 3 June 1963. (*Hugh Ballantyne*)

Voigtlander CLR   f2.8 Skopar
Agfa CT18   f8, 1/60

Left: A portrait of one of the 139 Class 3P 2–6–2T passenger tank locomotives which Mr Stanier introduced in 1935. Basically they were a domeless taper boiler version of the 1930 series of Fowler 2–6–2Ts, but it seems that in service they were not regarded as one of Stanier's best designs. Be that as it may, their range of duties was wide and they could be found all over the LMS system. Here, No 40148 stands in the yard at Holbeck shed, Leeds, between spells of empty coaching stock duties around Leeds City station. This engine was built at Derby in 1937 and was one of six in the class which was given a larger 6B boiler in an attempt to improve performance. This boiler was fitted in 1942 and the engine was withdrawn in September 1962, the final year in which any of the class remained at work. 23 September 1960. (*G W Morrison*)
Zeiss Contaflex   f2.8 Tessar   Agfa CT18

Below: The last generation of LMS locomotive design manifests itself here in the shape of H G Ivatt's light Class 2P 2–6–2T which became an LMS standard class. The first appeared in 1946 and eventually, by 1952, 130 had been built, some of which went to work on the Southern and Western Regions. Seen here is No 41222, built in 1948, which was for many years a regular performer on the Wolverton–Newport Pagnell branch right up to its closure on 4 September 1964, when she also worked the last branch train before moving north. The low winter sunlight shows the pleasing lines of No 41222, looking smart in lined black livery, and busy on pilot duty at the south end of Carlisle station. 13 February 1965. (*Hugh Ballantyne*)
Voigtlander CLR   f2.8 Skopar
Agfa CT18   f8, 1/60

When W A Stanier became CME in 1932 he wasted no time in setting about dealing with the company's motive power problems. Within 17 months of taking office, the first Stanier-designed locomotive entered traffic on 1 July 1933. This was No 6200, the first of the 'Princess Royal' class Pacifics for express passenger work. These Pacifics were introduced for the Anglo-Scottish services and the two prototypes included domeless taper Belpaire boilers with low temperature superheat and top feed. It was this small superheat which was to prove troublesome under LMS operating conditions, and when the further batch of ten engines, numbered 6203-12, was built at Crewe in 1935 these locomotives had a modified boiler with shorter tubes and a larger firebox. They became eminently successful locomotives but were gradually overshadowed by the work of the 'Princess Coronations' although, like the later Pacifics, they were of most handsome appearance, as evidenced here in the shape of No 46206 *Princess Marie Louise* standing at Crewe in 1961, a year before she was withdrawn from service. (*Basil Roberts*)
Kodak Retinette 1B   Agfa CT18

A fine vintage action picture of 'Princess Royal' Class Pacific No 46207 *Princess Arthur of Connaught* picking up water off Castlethorpe troughs, two miles north of Wolverton and 54 miles from Euston. These were one of six such sets of troughs from which the engine could obtain water en route from Liverpool Lime Street to Euston, a distance of 193½ miles. The red livery of the Pacific blends well with its train which, with the neat front nameboard on the engine, adds a final touch of glamour to the up 'Merseyside Express' on its non-stop run to London. 30 August 1958. (*T B Owen*)
Leica 3c   f2 85mm Sonnar
Kodachrome 8 ASA   f2.8, 1/200

Left: The cereal crop is ready for harvesting from the flat and fertile soil of the Warrington area of south Lancashire as one of the unusual-looking Stanier Class 5s No 44686 approaches Winwick Junction and prepares to take the Manchester line with an unidentified summer Saturday train from the North Wales coast route. Although the Class 5s eventually reached the substantial total of 842 locomotives, they were never so highly standardised as the more numerous old LNWR DX class or later WD type 2–8–0s. This engine is one of the visually most distinctive variations, readily apparent with its high running plate, massive outside steam pipes, double chimney and Caprotti valve gear. This locomotive and identical twin No 44687 were the last two Class 5s built, emerging from Horwich in April and May 1951. They each cost some £5000 more than the last orthodox Class 5, delivered from Horwich four months previously, the increase arising due to development charges, inflationary costs of labour and materials and the provision of SKF roller bearing axleboxes throughout. 24 August 1963. (*Hugh Ballantyne*)
Voigtlander CLR   f2.8 Skopar
Agfa CT18   f5.6, 1/125

Above: The very last new locomotive design of the LMS by H G Ivatt was his second and larger 2–6–0, classified 4F. This became a standard class, albeit of somewhat alien appearance to people in these islands due to the extremely high running plate with no drop plate in front of the cylinders, high cab and double chimney. The first three of the class emerged from Horwich by December 1947, just as the LMS chapter in history closed pending its compulsory nationalisation by the socialist government of the day on 1 January 1948. Eventually 162 engines were built and No 43019, built at Horwich in 1948, is seen in this picture at Preston coming off the remnant of the former Longridge branch and past the impressive LNWR Preston No 5 signal box on a trip working. Two weeks after the photograph was taken the engine was withdrawn from Lostock Hall shed. 28 March 1968. (*Hugh Ballantyne*)
Voigtlander CLR   f2.8 Skopar
Agfa CT18   f5.6, 1/250

The LNWR had a long secondary line which ran diagonally south-westwards through central Wales from Craven Arms to Llandovery and, partly by joint ownership, onwards to Carmarthen and Swansea Victoria. The line is, just, still open for dmu passenger trains to Llanelli but in steam days the mainstay service was at least five trains each way from Shrewsbury to Swansea, usually in the 1950–60s worked by LMS or BR Standard Class 5s. Shown here is Class 5 No 45145, built by Armstrong Whitworth in 1935, which has steam to spare as she arrives at Builth Road High Level with the 12 noon Shrewsbury–Swansea Victoria. This train was scheduled 4 hours 17 minutes for the 115¼ miles journey, in which there were no fewer than 26 stops. 20 April 1960. (*T B Owen*)
Leica 3c   f2 Summicron
Kodachrome 8 ASA   f4, 1/40

Left
No
sin
2.4
tra
off
lan
of
line
on
eng
sor
sta
loc

One of Fowler's Class 5XP, later 6P, 'Patriot' class express passenger engines makes a fine picture standing at Willesden shed in the low sunlight. Portrayed is No 45511 *Isle of Man*, built at Crewe in 1932 but no so named until 1938. The crest of the island above the nameplate is clearly visible. The 'Patriots' were built to provide a passenger engine with a wider route availability than the recently introduced 'Royal Scot' and which might do the work of the existing 'Claugh-tons' without incurring the same heavy maintenance and fuel costs of the older engines. Even the rebuilt large-boilered 'Claughtons' had not resolved this problem, so Sir Henry Fowler decided to put the 3-cylinder chassis of the 'Royal Scot' under the enlarged 'Claughton' boiler. The result was the two prototypes, classified 5XP, nominally rebuilt 'Claughtons', but in reality very little was retained. They proved superior in performance to the enlarged 'Claughtons', with repair costs averaging 50 per cent less than the older engines. Fifty more 'Patriots' were built between 1932–4 and proved satisfactory in service, but unfortunately none have been preserved. 29 August 1959. (*R C Riley*)

Agfa Super Silette   *f2 Solagon*
Kodachrome 8 ASA   *f8, 1/60*

Above: In Northamptonshire the M1 motorway, a creation of the late 1950s, parallels closely the original London & Birmingham Railway for one and a half miles and this picture shows the location shortly after the motorway had opened. By today's standards the motorway appears empty and even the forerunner of a service area sign looks quite antique! However, on the main line a Stanier Class 5 2–6–0 mixed traffic engine is hard at work on the slight down grade from Welton with a parcels train heading south, probably for Willesden or Euston. June 1960. (*D Cross*)
Canon VT6   f1.4 135mm Seremar

Right: At Stechford, in the eastern suburbs of Birmingham on the former LNWR main line to that city, one of Mr Stanier's Class 5 Moguls No 42957 is seen shunting in the goods yard. The class totalled 40 engines, all built at Crewe in 1933–4 to his new design produced by Horwich drawing office, but they were quite unlike the preceding and successful 245 'Crab' mixed traffic Moguls of Hughes/Fowler design. One of the class, No 42968, has been preserved and can be seen on the Severn Valley Railway. 14 June 1962. (*Michael Mensing*)
Kodak Retina 2A   f2 Xenon   Agfa CT18 f5, 1/250

Stanier's production of new designs and locomotives was prodigious following his appoint-
ment in January 1932 and by the end of 1935
there were 325 of his locomotives in service.
During that year Derby produced the first of a
handsome Class 4P 2–6–4T, a 2-cylinder version of his similar 3-cylinder type which had
been introduced in 1934 for the Southend line.
Here No 42663 stands early one morning by the
coaling stage at Uttoxeter shed, not long ex-
works. Sadly at that late date for steam it has
been returned to traffic in plain black livery
without the lining, but nevertheless still makes
an attractive sight. In all 206 of these engines
were built and distributed widely over the LMS
system. 29 August 1964. (*Hugh Ballantyne*)
Voigtlander CLR   f2.8 Skopar
Agfa CT18   f8, 1/60

The reliable Stanier 2–6–4T series shown opposite was multiplied when C E Fairburn introduced his modified updated version in 1945. This comprised a reduction of ten inches to 15 ft 4 in of the coupled wheelbase and lower working weight by over two tons to 85¼ tons, thus extending slightly the class's route availability. The only noticeable external difference was the austere look introduced by Fairburn in doing away with the footplate dropping in front of the cylinders and the bar section footsteps. However, they were good engines and became an LMS standard class. Like the Staniers they were widely dispersed over the system: indeed 41 of the total of 227 Fairburns were built at Brighton and used on the Southern Region. The picture shows the mid-afternoon van train from Leeds to Lancaster with No 42135 (built Derby in 1950), from Lancaster depot, passing Shipley on its way home. This train was of interest to local enthusiasts because of the variety of power which could be rostered, 'Patriots', 'Crabs' and the 2–6–4Ts often performing. 10 May 1961. (G W Morrison)

Zeiss Contaflex   *f2.8 Tessar*   *Perutz C18*

Above: A Class 5 on the Midland Railway's approach to Lancaster in the shape of No 45303 passing Ladies Walk signal box at Lancaster with the 5.02 pm train from Bradford (which combined with a Leeds portion at Skipton) to Morecambe. The train was at one time known as the 'Leeds, Bradford & Morecambe Residential Express' and this picture shows the return working of the 7.15 morning train heading to the coast. This service was for Bradford and Leeds businessmen and enabled them to live near the shores of Morecambe Bay but conveniently travel the 60 or so miles to their work in the major centres of the thriving and industrial West Riding. July 1964. (*N A Machell*)
Zeiss Werra   f2.8 Tessar   Agfa CT18 f4, 1/250

Right: On a cold winter day in 1964 Fowler Class 4F No 44389 pours smoke on to the overhead electric wires at Scale Hall, Lancaster, as she gets into her stride with the 12.40 Heysham–Tees Yard goods. The train is running under the electrified Lancaster–Morecambe–Heysham line which was then being used as a test line for 6.6 kV ac electrification. If you look closely at the overhead line structures you will see they are all different, having been erected by BICC and BR for experimental purposes. (*N A Machell*)
Zeiss Werra   f2.8 Tessar   Agfa CT18 f5.6, 1/250

Right: Although the first 113 'Jubilees' entered traffic unnamed in 1934–5, it was in keeping with the patriotic tradition of the LMS company's naming policy to commemorate the Silver Jubilee of HM King George V and Queen Mary in May 1935 by naming an engine *Silver Jubilee*. The locomotive chosen was not the existing first of the class, No 5552, but No 5642, which switched numbers. The new No 5552 was so named and henceforth the class became known as the 'Silver Jubilee' or simply 'Jubilee' class. The engines received names mainly comprising British Empire countries, various states within them and colonies, followed by admirals, famous sea battles, warships and a few odds and ends, making 191 names in all. Here one of the admirals, No 45647 *Sturdee*, roars up the 1 in 132 rise from Mickle Trafford to Guilden Sutton signal box, just east of Chester, with the 9.15 am Leeds–Llandudno train. 20 August 1966. *(Hugh Ballantyne)*
Voigtlander CLR   f2.8 Skopar
Agfa CT18   f4–5.6, 1/500

Opposite: The photographer is just about to get wet from the overflow off the tender as 'Jubilee' class No 45694 *Bellerophon* hurries over Salwick troughs near Preston on the LNWR/LYR Preston & Wyre joint line with the 1.35 pm (SO) Blackpool–Bradford train. Note that as long ago as 1966 BR reduced the line capacity by half to its present level as the two far tracks are disused. This had been a quadruple line, once carrying enormous railborne excursion traffic to Blackpool, one of the country's most famous seaside resorts. 9 July 1966. *(Hugh Ballantyne)*
Voigtlander CLR   f2.8 Skopar
Agfa CT18   f4, 1/500

With its maze of lines originally both LMS and LNER constituent company-owned, plus the multitude of private sidings of the brewery railways, Burton-on-Trent was a fascinating place for the railway enthusiast. This picture portrays the atmosphere of some of the sidings as Class 4F 0–6–0 No 44538 shunts wagons from Bass & Co malthouses at Shobnall Junction back towards the main line, whilst Bass diesel No 6 (a Baguley 204 hp locomotive) looks on before moving off with a couple of malt wagons. Note the lovely array of Midland lower quadrant signals, and the Midland signal box protecting the level crossing in the background. 4 June 1963. (*Hugh Ballantyne*)
Voigtlander CLR   f2.8 Skopar
Agfa CT18   f8, 1/125

An engine type which needs no introduction and was the embodiment of Midland locomotive influence seen throughout the LMS and London Midland Region. This Fowler-designed Class 4F 0–6–0 originally comprised 192 units on the Midland Railway by the time of the grouping in 1923. Subsequently the LMS built another 575 and acquired five more from the SDJR in 1930, making a class total of 772 locomotives. Their mainstay work was goods haulage, as seen here, but they frequently worked passenger trains as well. One of the 1925 Derby-built locomotives No 44044, from Stourton shed, rumbles past Wortley Junction, Leeds, with a coal train bound for Kirkstall power station. 14 March 1962. (*G W Morrison*)
Zeiss Contaflex   f2.8 Tessar   Agfa CT18

An interesting picture contrasting the extremes of size in the LMS post-war standard classes. After working 1M32, a Saturdays only Glasgow to Morecambe train, 'Princess Coronation' Pacific No 46241 *City of Edinburgh* returns down the main line to Carnforth shed for servicing in company with a humble Class 3F 0–6–0T No 47375, which was also going back to Carnforth after a spell of shunting duty at Heysham Harbour. The two locomotives are seen having just come off the Bare Lane to Hest Bank spur and on to the West Coast Main Line at Hest Bank, proceeding backwards away from the photographer. July 1964. (*N A Machell*)
Zeiss Werra   f2.8 Tessar   Agfa CT18 f5.6, 1/250

A reminder of an important but unadvertised function of railway operation in the steam era. Banking of trains was required in many areas and on the West Coast Main Line Tebay was famous as the home of the bankers required to assist trains up the hill to Shap summit, which included a section of more than four miles up a 1 in 75 gradient. For many years Fowler 2–6–4Ts were the mainstay bankers but later, Fairburn 2–6–4Ts were drafted in, as seen here in the shape of No 42210, in unlined black livery, giving a northbound goods train a hard push out of Tebay and on to the 1 in 75 upgrade. 25 August 1966. (*Alan Trickett*)
Canon L1   Agfa CT18   f4, 1/500

Left: Just past the halfway mark up the 1 in 75 climb to Shap near Scout Green signal box 'Jubilee' No 45713 *Renown* is going well with the 2.15 pm Liverpool Exchange–Glasgow Central train. Note the engine is attached to a Fowler tender. 11 August 1962. (*Hugh Ballantyne*)
Voigtlander CLR   f2.8 Skopar
Agfa CT18   f4, 1/500

Above: The author used to make long and time-consuming journeys to the Shap area from his home at Bath and soon learnt that it was a waste of time to rely on weather forecasts applicable to the north of England because Shap had a fickle and temperamental weather pattern all of its own, just as Ais Gill seems to have today! The only consistent feature was the lack of sunshine at the critical moment, and this picture is one of very few I ever managed to take here of a train in sunshine. Class 5 No 44727, one of ten Class 5s constructed with a steel firebox, and built at Crewe in 1949, is seen at Shap Wells with the down 'Lakes Express', 11.35 am Euston–Workington. 29 August 1964. (*Hugh Ballantyne*)
Voigtlander CLR   f2.8 Skopar
Agfa CT18   f4, 1/500

Above: The largest constituent company formed into the LMS on 1 January 1923 was the London & North Western Railway which, like the other constituents, had its own fleet of locomotives of distinctive design and appearance. This picture shows the functional lines of one of that company's heavy goods type and the last class of LNWR engine to see service on BR, Class 7F 0-8-0 No 49125 in ex-works condition near its birthplace, on Crewe South shed. 21 October 1961. (*G W Morrison*)
Zeiss Contaflex   f2.8 Tessar   Agfa CT18

Right: In the evening of her days a work-weary LNWR G2a series 0-8-0 of power class 7F, No 49173 is seen one morning shunting near her home depot at Bushbury, Wolverhampton. A year later she was withdrawn, as were the few remaining LNWR 0-8-0s from nearby Bescot shed, the last two working until a day or two before Christmas 1964. Fortunately one, No 49395, the first of the Beames series of G2 class, has been preserved and now resides out of service on display at Ironbridge, Shropshire. 24 August 1963. (*Hugh Ballantyne*)
Voigtlander CLR   f2.8 Skopar
Agfa CT18   f8, 1/30

Left: On a hot Saturday in July 'Jubilee' No 45685 *Barfleur*, complete with London Midland Region style headboard, but with stock mostly finished in WR chocolate and cream livery, speeds northwards past Coaley Junction station in Gloucestershire with 'The Devonian', 9.30 am Paignton–Bradford express. 7 July 1962. (*Michael Mensing*)
Hasselblad 1000F
f2.8 Tessar   Ektachrome
f3.8, 1/1000

Opposite: Class 8F 2–8–0 No 48745, an example built to LNER order at Darlington in 1946, brings a Sunday morning coal train through the cutting just north of Bredon in south Worcestershire on 28 November 1965. This was one of a number of Sunday trains run at this period from Saltley, Birmingham to the Western Region. Some of these ran via the Honeybourne line but whichever route was used, the engine was taken off the train at Gloucester and despatched northwards again, often light engine, since by this time the WR was almost completely dieselised and steam was certainly not welcome in its territory. (*John H Dagley-Morris*)
Kodak Retinette
Agfa CT18
f6.5, 1/250

Above: Recently ex-works from Crewe in the early 1960s, a resplendent 'Converted Royal Scot' No 46148 *The Manchester Regiment* rests briefly at Stafford shed during a running-in diagram which has brought her on local passenger trains from Crewe via Shrewsbury and Newport, Shropshire, before turning and heading north back down the main line to the starting point. (*J B Bucknall*)
Pentax S1   f2 Takumar   Agfa CT18

Right: The driver is keeping a sharp lookout as he brings 'Converted Royal Scot' No 46136 *The Border Regiment* over Bushey troughs, 15 miles north-west of Euston, on the last stages of the journey up to London with an FA Cup special for Wembley. 7 May 1960. (*T B Owen*)
Leica 3c   85 mm f2 Sonnar
Kodachrome 8 ASA   f2.6, 1/125

Tebay shed (last BR shed code 12E) by night, three days before steam finished working here. Inside can be seen three of the Standard Class 4 4–6–0s which were sent there during 1967 to replace 2–6–4Ts on banking duties up to Shap, but they only lasted until the end of the year, when Clayton Type 1 900 hp diesels took over. The shed closed on 1 January 1968. 28 December 1967. (L A Nixon)
Exakta Varex IIa   85mm Biometer
Kodachrome II   f4, 2 mins

Willesden, showing the original LNWR 12-road shed with three hipped roofs designed by Mr J Ramsbottom and built in 1873, although the engines visible in the foreground stand on the site of a later Webb extension which was removed in 1939 after a roundhouse (see page 42) had been constructed in 1929 behind the old sheds. This important depot was closed completely on 27 September 1965 and subsequently demolished. The site now forms part of the Willesden Freightliner terminal. 10 June 1964. (*Hugh Ballantyne*)

Voigtlander CLR   f2.8 Skopar
Agfa CT18   f8, 1/60

Above: One of Sir Henry Fowler's successful 'Patriot' Class 5XP (later Class 6P) 4–6–0s No 45510 from Lancaster shed, going well near Harrison's Sidings, north of Shap, with a Crewe to Carlisle parcels train. This engine (a nominal rebuild of an old 'Claughton' No 6012) was built at Crewe in 1932 and was one of ten out of a class total of 52 never to receive a name. It was withdrawn in June 1962 and cut up at its birthplace in August of the same year. 6 August 1960.

(G W Morrison)
Zeiss Contaflex   *f2.8 Tessar*   *Agfa CT18*

Right: Rather less glamorous work for a main line Pacific but a revenue-earning job all the same for 'Princess Coronation' No 46240 *City of Coventry*, as this impressive engine pulls out of the up loop at Carnforth to head south with a Carlisle to London Broad Street meat train. 10 June 1964. *(Noel A Machell)*
Zeiss Werra   *f2.8 Tessar*   *Agfa CT18*

One of the little Johnson Class 2F 0–6–0s No 58143 from Coalville shed working a goods train on the West Bridge, Leicester to Desford Junction branch passing the closed station at Glenfield. For many years engines of this class were retained to work the line as they were sufficiently small to pass through the narrow bore of the 1796 yards long Glenfield tunnel, just visible in the background. The Class 2Fs reigned until December 1963 when they were replaced by slightly modified Standard Class 2 2–6–0s. No 58143 was a member of the Midland '1142' class built in 1875–6 by contractors. During the course of their long lives most of them were rebuilt with G6 boilers, new frames and Deeley cabs. The branch formed part of the Leicester & Swannington Railway, which was one of the earliest steam-operated railways in England, the first in the Midland Shires and the oldest component of the Midland Railway. It opened throughout for passenger traffic on 27 April 1833, passenger traffic continuing on the West Bridge to Desford section until 24 September 1928, while goods services survived through the Beeching era, the last train running on 29 April 1966. 4 May 1962. (*R C Riley*)
Agfa Super Silette   f2 Solagon
Kodachrome II   f4, 1/250

Further south in Midland territory there was a 14-mile branch line off the Birmingham–Bristol line at Ashchurch which went westwards to Tewkesbury, then bridged the River Severn to reach Upton-on-Severn and Malvern Wells, where it connected with the GWR Worcester–Hereford line. The branch was first cut back to Upton-on-Severn and finally closed to passengers on 12 August 1961. At the quiet little Worcestershire village station of Ripple, a popular destination for fisherman, Midland Class 3F No 43520 pauses with the 1.30 pm (SO) from Upton to Tewkesbury one summer day in 1959, by which time the service was down to only three weekday and five Saturday trains. The engine was originally a Johnson '1798' class 0–6–0 dating from 1888 and subsequently rebuilt with a Belpaire G7 type boiler. The final survivors of this useful class were not withdrawn until February 1964. 25 July 1959. (T B Owen)

Leica 3c   f2 Summicron
Kodachrome 8 ASA   f2.6, 1/200

Standard Class 9F 2–10–0 No 92110, one of the ultimate British heavy goods (and general purpose) engines, seen running over the backbone of England along the 1100 feet contour between Garsdale and Ais Gill. The 9F is bringing a Blackburn to Long Meg Sidings (north of Appleby) empty mineral wagon train out of the 106-yard Tunnel No 124, known as Shotlock Tunnel. 17 July 1965. (*John H Dagley-Morris*) *Kodak Retinette   Agfa CT18   f6.5, 1/250*

Except for the BR official last steam special train on Sunday 11 August 1968 the last steam day to all intents and purposes was Sunday 4 August 1968. Here on that Sunday morning the two engines booked to work the RCTS 'End of Steam Commemorative Rail Tour' wait at Manchester Victoria for the 600 participants to arrive from Euston, which they did, somewhat late. Obviously both locomotives were in the very last batch of withdrawals by BR in August 1968. Standard Class 5 No 73069 of Carnforth and

Stanier Class 8F No 48476 from Lostock Hill shed took the special train through south Lancashire to Blackburn on a circuitous route via Oldham and Bolton, thence to Hellifield, Skipton, Burnley and back through Blackburn to Lostock Hall, Preston, where these two engines finished their working lives. The tour then returned to Manchester behind No 70013 *Oliver Cromwell*. 4 August 1968. (*Peter J C Skelton*) *Mamiya C3   Agfa CT18   f5.6–8, 1/125*

To conclude here is a picture of what many people consider to be Sir William Stanier's finest steam locomotive design, photographed on 'foreign' soil, but paradoxically rather appropriate, as it shows 'Princess Coronation' No 46251 *City of Nottingham* standing outside Swindon shed. It was here that Stanier had so ably trained for his profession under the influence of Messrs Churchward and Collett, and eventually become one of our greatest locomotive engineers. The Pacific had worked an RCTS special 'The East Midlander No 7 Rail Tour' from Nottingham Victoria for members to visit Eastleigh and Swindon Works, taking the train to Didcot via the GCR main line to Woodford Halse, thence to Banbury. No 46251 ran light to Swindon to await the train on its return from Hampshire before going back to Nottingham by the same route. 9 May 1964. (*Hugh Ballantyne*)
Voigtlander CLR   f2.8 Skopar
Agfa CT18   f8, 1/60